Intimate Emotions

By: Leonard L. Leitzel

To order additional copies of this book, contact:
Xlibris
844-714-8691
www.Xlibris.com
Orders@Xlibris.com

ISBN: Softcover   978-1-6698-0896-1
          EBook   978-1-6698-0895-4

Print information available on the last page

Rev. date: 01/28/2022

Intimate Emotions

My Grandparents

They gave of their lives in pure delight, to serve
their master and do what is right.
In seasons past, they gave their best, leaving
examples for all the rest.
Oh, God above, to you we raise, our gratitude
and solemn praise.
You gave to us a grand reward of Christian
love from up above.
You've given wisdom in parenthood to raise our
children, as we should.
We dedicate them all to you, so you can show
us what to do;
For this we give you all our praise and vow to
serve you all our days.
When we were weak, you gave us grace to
surge ahead and see your face.
I see a smile on their face, a glow of warmth
and godly grace.
Lord, gives to us a faith like theirs, so we can
train our younger heirs:
For treasures here cannot abound, unless we're
standing on Holy Ground.
Again we give you everything and praise you
as our mighty king.

A Piercing Beacon

In the dark and all alone is a

beacon of light upon a stone.

Reflections are seen across the waves,

giving a glimpse of onshore caves.

Jagged and broken, the shores are a trap,

for sailors and vessels destroyed in one snap.

With wind in the sails and courage in

hand, our captain will guide us away from

the land.

Take heart and don't fear, the dark will subside.

Keep watch in this hour; we're in for a ride.

In a flash of a moment, a beacon gives light,

sending its message in the darkest of nights.

Passing Iris

A deep impression one can only explain,

It passes the iris and then fills the brain.

Responding right after, any fool will tell,

leaves little time to consider if we have

done well.

In search for our answers, we've all

fallen short, for finding directions

we all must sort.

So from our brain we process our lives,

cutting through problems like very sharp

knives.

In these passing moments, we often do

shun, the answer were given through

God's only son.

If only we'd taken the solution he

gave, all could be given, and

our lives he would save.

A Solitary Teardrop

In a moment like this, I search for a sign to
express to you a new gift that is mine. It was
given to me by someone who cared. Her
patience and love with her soul she has bared.

To the family that I've left behind, my
prayer would be that you grow up precious
and kind, for you never can tell whose life
you may touch when sharing with them about
the God who loves them so much.

My daughters are precious to me; I loved
them so much, as all could see. To them I
would say, take heart and be strong. I will
see you one day in glory above and express
to you there my unending love.

Bitter Air

A suffocating breeze came through the trees; to

take a breath could bring sudden death.

Down on my knees in search for air,

seeking the oxygen with urgent care.

My eyes are burning with the toxins of smoke,

as the air in my lung makes me violently choke.

A burst of fresh air is such a surprise,

a precious gift which money can't buy.

To each one is given but a moment to

live, search for the reason, but then you

must give. The reason for sharing is so

someone can be, eternally blessed for all

eternity.

Higher Dreams

I wished for a new day, and what I did see

was a glimpse of a moment when I would

feel free. I carry some burdens, I've

had for a while, although I might worry,

you may see me smile.

I know there's a new day that is written in gold,

and its solid promise has no other mold.

When solving your questions, you might often ask,

for finding all reason can be a great task.

However, I wonder if opinions will do,

for wisdom is held by only a few.

How often I ponder what reason exist,

when questions are answered with a

dark, dreary mist.

Be aware of the answer that governs your choice.

Good answers still come in a very small voice.

Destinies Road

I walked along a road worn with age.
Its surface structure had seen many a
stage. One moment its transport was
heavy and loud, the next but a mere
passing croud.
Today this road lies all alone,
abused by time as history has
shone. As I walk along its
earth, I tend to wonder of
its worth. Erosion takes a toll
with time, when men do toil to
make a dime. Though in a hurry
our time will end; our passage in
life we all shall spend. To this
degree, we must not wait to patch
the roads that seal our fate.

Submissive Submersion

In each heart, there's a yearning from deep

within, to dense and vanquish all our sin.

We came here today to show you our love

and all of our praise to our Father above.

Your faith is in things that are yet to be seen,

when all else crumbles on him we can lean.

Today is a day of special reserve,

your giving your life to the one you will serve.

His promise he gives to fit all your needs,

submerge in his love, and he'll rid your old deeds.

Resurface to find your life is renewed, to serve

your new master and feed on his food.

In eating the manna from heaven above,

we nourish our bodies with his unending love.

Now from this moment that you are set free,

I urge you to follow his royal decree.

Identity

Forever searching but can't seem to find

the treasures I've sought with my

overworked mind.

Looking for legends that do not exist

is like looking for mountains in the

early morning mist.

I'm taken aback by what I have lost,

willing to find it no matter the cost.

True love is art that continues to grow

even when artists are painting it slow.

When painting our portrait, the

colors we use will give the impressions,

for those who will choose.

My colors will always be honest and true; all

others will blot and then turn blue.

Failing Sight

Amidst the clouds of blue, my thoughts

return to you. The moments we

once had can make me very sad.

I held you long ago, deep in this

heart of mine, and in those passing

moments I did not see you go.

Your heart was prone to wander as I

was soon to find, if only you could

know the pain you left behind.

I always gave you the love I had; I

never thought it was so bad.

I know this time will pass on through.

I'll gain my strength, then start anew.

A better place is mine to find. I

wished you hadn't been so blind.

Eternal Night

Fear the coming day when evil men will pay.

Hearts will beat in fear for what they all

shall here.

Time shall still remain with nothing

left to gain.

Yet memories will survive to add some grief

and pain, feeding all their torture,

before they go insane.

Death no longer lingers for those who

could not see. Eternal night has started,

from this they cannot flee.

Prayer Stones

In a box are some very special rocks; each carries

a name and a burden of the same.

Some are big, and others are small, but all are

rounded like a ball. The reason for these I now

must tell; they represent souls to save from hell.

I'll pray for each with special care,

for they all need a better fare.

Out of the box in silence they stare, awaiting

the prayers we all should bear.

Today it's a rock, tomorrow a soul, each one

will carry a mighty great toll.

Small but heavy, solid and round, a stone for

a box can always be found. Remember

the prayers of every kind, and don't

be hasty to rid them of mind.

Printed in the United States
by Baker & Taylor Publisher Services